MW00640216

ATAANA BADILLI

CALLING MY POWER BACK TO ME

ISBN 978-1-09830-931-2 eBook 978-1-09830-932-9

ATAANA BADILLI

At an early age, Ataana experienced an awakening to God's presence and the Oneness in all of existence and knew that he would assist others in their awakening process and healing journey. Ataana immersed himself in the study of healing, world religions, shamanism, spirituality, psychology, and everything related to the mind, body, soul, and the mysteries of existence. Ataana awoke to deep inner visions that allowed him to see and understand future and present projections based on energy flow and everything and everyone around him. He also understood complex multidimensional patterns of karma and morphogenetic fields.

He gained access to the Oneness and Multidimensionality of realities. It was perfectly normal for Ataana to see past and parallel lives. It was also intrinsic for him to intuitively apply transformational energy when required. The deep mysteries of life fascinated and guided Ataana in a way that transformed him into a mystic himself, and he soon combined his spiritual insights with learned knowledge. The definition of a mystic describes Ataana's journey substantially: a person who seeks, through contemplation and self-surrender, to obtain unity with the absolute.

At the age of twenty, God's energy was amplified in and around Ataana for seven days, prompting him to devote his life to Spiritual healing work and to becoming a teacher and healer. On his ensuing journey, he experienced suffering, unhealthy patterns, addictions, human trauma, disconnection from source, dysfunctional behaviors, beauty of friendship, life, love, and the quest and realization of enlightenment. A profound purification process at the age of twenty-seven led him to embark on formal studies in natural medicine. Ataana attended naturopathic schools in Germany in cities such as Berlin and Cologne and was later initiated into shamanism and other healing modalities. From then on, Ataana supported healing and transformation wherever he traveled and volunteered his services until he became a spiritual teacher.

The rise of consciousness and living our fullest potential comprise the core of Ataana's teachings. Energy and transformational work allow us to remember how to live in balance with all of creation. Ataana inspires us to tune in, activate, and access all of our energy to unveil our highest and unfeigned light. Part of the process is connecting the self-conscious to the so called Source and to pursuing the spiritual journey at whatever point we are on in our path and to whatever faith we belong. Over the years, Ataana developed unique healing methods, called the Sacred Inner Dialogue (SID) and the Ataana Healing Method, and established a healing center in Nashville, Tennessee, with the Nashville Crystal Store where he shares his gifts in personal sessions, workshops on Energy Works Radio, and Let's Talk Healing. He is also known for his Prosperity Mantras and for cameos on television. More information can be found at www.ataanamethod.com.

This is the second publication in which Ataana Badilli shares his spiritual wisdom and metaphysical experiences, and another one of his powerful tools for self-healing:

Calling All of My Power Back to Me.

CHAPTER 1

Calling All of Your Power Back to Yourself

I call all of my power back to me. I am whole and complete.

Multidimensional energy recovery,

Where intention goes, energy goes.

All of the power that we still hold onto from other people actually holds us back from moving forward when we use these energies as crutches because we think that we can't do it by ourselves. If we don't believe in our wholeness, we don't believe that we are unlimited energy systems, and that we can succeed in life.

Now please state with me (three times, with intent, these following two sentences):

1. I return all the power that doesn't belong to me.

2. All of the power that I'm still holding onto from other people that doesn't belong to me, I now send back.

Now repeat the following sentences thrice with a strong intent:

"I call all of my own power back to me. I am whole and complete."

Two more times.

In the following Paragraph, I show you an exercise, share with you the scripts, the Energy words to apply, and address why it is of eminent importance to send the power that doesn't belong to us back from where we took it, and for us to retrieve all of our power from whoever took it from us or we gave it to.

Let me start by showing you the hand movements for this exercise which accompany the words, "I call all of my power back to me. I am whole and complete."

1. Begin this exercise with both arms extended horizontally (parallel to the ground). Your palms are facing forward.

2. As you speak, "I call all of my power back to me," bend your arms and bring your hands together between your heart chakra (Anahata) and the solar plexus chakra (Manipura). While moving your hands to the Anahata, close your hands as you slowly pull your power back to yourself.

Note: Your focus is the Anahata since your power, emotional/spiritual energy, and your life force resonate the most with the Anahata or heart chakra.

3. Bring both hands close together so that they touch.

4. Now move your hands apart and extend the left hand toward the sky and your right hand toward the ground.

5. Bring your hands together once more at your Anahata. While moving your hands to the Anahata, close your hands slowly and say, "I am whole and complete."

6. Conclude this exercise by opening your arms and hands once more. Stand in gratitude and in awareness of your power returning with your arms extended, open and relaxed, and hands pointing forward.

When doing these exercises, repeat them three times for optimal results.

CHAPTER 2

Why Will We Benefit from This Exercise?

Why should we regularly call all of our power back and send the power that doesn't belong to us back to where we got it from? It will help us to be more present and non-parasitic in our prosperity and energy awareness. Calling all of our power back to us is so extraordinarily important with respect to our present, future, as well as to any past life, or any dimension in which we may still have an unhealthy energy attachment. Just think about all of our past experiences, good or bad, that leave us in nostalgia and take our focus from this very moment away. This exercise allows us to recognize and resolve all of our unhealthy energy investments. In order to understand the full scope of it, it is important to know that each time we remember an unresolved past traumatic experience, WE ARE SENDING OUT ENERGY, which is usually our energy.

What we are doing in this moment is literally sending our life force in the direction and time of the unresolved traumatic experience and the person or group that we co-created it with, even if it was years ago. When we send our energy in that direction, and we are not receiving a balanced return, meaning a return of energy that matches our energy investment in its quality of high vibration, then it is an energy loss. If we are consciously or subconsciously sending our energy to a place (situation, person, etc.) from where we do not receive a positive return, or do not know exactly what we are getting in return, we need an action-tool that supports us to get our full life force back, and send the life force that we hold onto from others back to them.

Let me explain this part further.

We are all unlimited energy systems. Now, if we are not feeling our full potential in this, and every moment, the question is, who is doing what with it? This question regarding how our energy is used is a crucial one. Whenever you are not in conscious control of all your life force, your energy could potentially be used by others for noble or ill purposes. Your energy can be attached to these deeds just like DNA left on a crime scene, and the karmic responsibility for these actions can be traced back to you since it's your energy. Therefore, not being in your full power is about more than simply not feeling well! Reclaiming all of your power is a form of energy hygiene and energy prosperity; it allows you to be in better charge of actions, including avoiding the ones which could create unwanted repercussions or karma.

What I am sharing here with you is a way in which you can reclaim your power at all times.

As I have explained, being in command of all our creative energy is more optimal than sending our energy to a place from which we do not know if we will receive a positive return. Is our energy focus creating something useful or unhealthy? We have to ask ourselves this on a regular basis to know whether we are indeed in our full power of creation. Everything we create without being in command of our full power is compromised, since we can create what we desire to the extent to which we have access to our energy or power.

Let me explain the process of creation under compromised and ideal conditions with an analogy. Our life force of creation is like an electromagnet running on a certain percentage of its overall capacity. An electromagnet runs at, let us say, fifty percent of its capacity. What is happening is that it can, under these compromised conditions, only attract fifty percent of its magnetic potential. If the electromagnetic force is reduced, then as a consequence, it doesn't run at one hundred percent but only on fifty percent of its maximum capacity; it is not able to attract the full extent of what it could be attracting. Similarly, if our creative energy is running only at fifty percent, what we are attracting can be limited as well, and will yield a return of only fifty percent. I want to make sure to emphasize this point.

Whenever we put our intention on a desired outcome, we want to focus our intention on that desired outcome with our full potential, with our full force of creation, in order to receive the maximum results. If projects and goals are not coming to full fruition, it would benefit us to regain full access to our inherent power before attempting again.

We must be in our full power to attract fully what we want to attract. If we set an intention with, say, twenty percent life force, we will be unable to fully manifest our desired outcome except if the outcome only requires a twenty percent focus. Therefore, calling our energy back regularly is important, whether we are doing energy work professionally or otherwise living our everyday lives. We want to ensure that we are in full command of our power so that we can achieve what we want to achieve to its fullest potential.

If someone does something a hundred percent, we know it and feel it. Also, our intuition tells us when we or someone else does something "half ass," or not one hundred percent (forgive my French here). The same concept applies to the creative energy and focus that we put into our intentions. The Universe might say, "Why don't you do this at one hundred percent?" The Universe will not rebuke us. However, it will simply deliver what we are asking for in exact relation to our force of focus and intention.

When I talk about "calling all of your power back to yourself and returning the power that doesn't belong to you," I mean becoming one hundred percent present in your own life force. Being present means, all of your life force is present at this time on this planet, in your body, and consciously accessible in this moment. The more present you are, the more presence you have, and the more consciousness is present, the more likely your order is being received by the Universe with infallible precision and also delivered to you. The more life force you contain, the more magnetic you are and the more effortlessly you attract what is yours. It is very important to understand that energy also means consciousness. Energy can provide fuel for heightened consciousness. That is why we are basically calling our consciousness, our presence, back to us whenever we call our power back.

Let me repeat: we are more present in this very moment. This means the more life force we have, the more magnetic we are, and the more effortlessly we attract that which we desire, the more awareness we have access to.

The action of calling all of our power back to us brings our awareness, and our presence, to our fullest holistic potential. It maximizes our focus, gives us the freedom to make better choices, and leads us to experience the wholeness of our being.

Our journey in life is to remember our fullest potential.

We, often unconsciously, do not want to be fully present because we've had experiences in our lives that were painful. Out of self-protection, we do not want to bear the presence of our painful memories. But the life energy tied up in those experiences, in trauma or pain, remains missing and not available for living life to our fullest potential. If we do not address and heal those issues, then all that energy remains not accessible to us.

Becoming conscious and reclaiming all our energy by healing our pain is the path to becoming fully present. This is why this exercise is so vital for us. Our being is many-layered—multidimensional. The longer we live, the more layers and experiences we accumulate in all dimensions.

That is why it is so important to know where the painful or traumatizing aspects of our selves are still running in memory loops after hours, weeks, or even years, and why experiences from the past keep resurfacing in our present lives. If we do not call our power that is tied up in those experiences back to us, then hundreds or thousands of loops spinning from the past can create fragmentation in our lives. As a consequence, parts of our energy are displaced one percent here, half a percent over there, 0.8 percent there, and so on. All of this may add up between forty to fifty percent of our total life force being fragmented.

The traumatic experiences in our past are like spinning wheels. They do not have to be "big" traumatic experiences like sexual abuse or a harsh upbringing. They could range from the seemingly trivial being embarrassed, not getting the bike you wanted to the more significant walking to school five or ten miles, not having enough food, or having abusive parents. It can be anything from not getting designer clothing to not having enough love or support to being abused.

Past traumatic experiences are negatively charged; they are most likely spinning and establishing more unhealthy patterns. You think back to them and you simply do not feel good. You look back and say, "That was a heavy experience," but every time you think of them, you are sending energy, life force, into those experiences.

Often we do not consciously know that we are actually feeling them because if you don't want to be reminded of something, your system pushes it down to the subconsciousness that still repeats the loop. You are recharging the trauma and providing new "energy fuel" for its continuation. On a daily or weekly basis, life force is being directed into those patterns. Trauma truly becomes more and more disturbing over a long period of time if not attended to and transformed.

Consider a scenario in which you are walking where there is no path. When you walk there again, you make a little track. If you walk more and more repeatedly on it, it becomes a trail. The more you travel on that little trail, the deeper it is ingrained in nature. The same thing happens when we replay traumatic experiences from the past; they become ingrained in our brains. This is also true for new positive habit-forming patterns. We create energy pathways.

Our ingrained paths also have an effect on the outside world. People find your path and say, "Oh, there's a path here. Let me walk on it, too." And they are motivated to take advantage of you like an instruction manual that you offer the world on how to treat you, since you are harboring these patterns. Parts of that unhealthy trail are being used by other patterns or energies as well, and they are further deepening the traumatic experience. When we deepen that experience, more and more energy is being directed toward it. Over ten years, this traumatic experience might receive so much energy, it could add a whole new dimension to the trauma.

Let me repeat: these paths are also being utilized as instruction manuals by other people on how to treat you. If you punish yourself by constantly going back to traumatic experiences, they may try to make you feel guilty or punish you as well, since that's what you are signaling to the Universe.

When I say, "I call all of my power back," I am calling my power back from these traumatic experiences, from these repetitive, refueling, reinforcing, unhealthy frequencies that are creating trails where there should be intact nature.

This is not merely a simple little exercise. This exercise is life-transforming and life-changing. When properly done, with the full intention of reclaiming our energy, it truly calls the life force and personal power that is trapped in traumatic experiences back, and forwards it to us. Notice the far-reaching effect of this exercise.

I am not calling my power back just because it sounds good, or because yesterday I noticed that I was not fully conscious. No, I am calling my power back from all past life experiences and experiences from my present life that still run traumatic patterns to do my part and be more whole.

I invite you to speak these words with sincere desire:

"I call all of my power back to me. I am whole and complete
I call all of my power back to me. I am whole and complete.
I call all of my power back to me. I am whole and complete."

Is there anything more cause-worthy than healing? The choice of reclaiming your power is a choice of self-healing and self-empowerment; that in itself changes your path. It does not matter what your karmic life was in the past. It does not matter in what direction it was going. Calling all of your power back to you is a statement that is put out there for the Universe to listen to. This is meaningful. This is you asking for something big, for something transformative, for something healing. In this moment, you are born, you arrived.

Consciousness awakens when you say these words. This is the depth underneath the obvious words. This is the frequency of the consciousness behind and underneath the words, "I call all of my power back to me. I am whole and complete." This is the very consciousness that is underneath, anchored by this combination of words. For example, it is like being affected by dreams, traffic, or subliminal messaging on the news, on TV, and movies into which we unintentionally send our power and life force. Just think about what the daily news and politics does to people and their emotional and mental states. With this exercise, we call our power and life force back from traffic, news, movies, dream state and cyberspace as well.

If you look at the programming that the reclaiming of your power creates, you discover a specific frequency that counteracts all the unhealthy programs that have been applied to you to keep you suppressed or sidetracked. I am sharing with you here, a specific tool to get you out of the system that is not beneficial to you.

"I call all of my power back to me. I am whole and complete." This is an intention. When you state it, you might not be totally in your full power yet, but you are in the process of gaining it, and the more you repeat it, the more you are gaining back your power with your full presence, and the more powerful you become.

When you start to call your power back, you may be running at thirty percent. You call more power back, and you may be at forty percent and then at fifty percent. The more you repeat this, the more you realize how compromised you were in your power. You then have access to an internal measuring device that tells you where you are at any given moment like a gauge. Moreover, by clearly seeing where you are standing, you can now ask yourself, "Am I currently in my full power or in a state of powerlessness?" Then you can adjust to the desired frequency by applying this system.

It is important for all of us to have a reference point, because without conscious training, we do not know where we are with our energy. For example, I can see where people are at in their lives and what percentage of power they are running on. I can look at a person and say if that person is running on only twenty percent. "This person is only about twenty percent in her or his overall power." This person might say, "Well, I tried this and that, and I only get twenty percent of what I am asking for in life." I say, "No surprise."

I do not mean this in a dismissive way, but it makes sense. Some of us are basically only twenty percent present. I know how that feels because I experienced these states of reduced consciousness on my own journey, but by applying the techniques that I share with you in these pages, I got myself out of them. It is important for all of us to know how to use this system because many people are trapped in unhealthy/dysfunctional situations and patterns even though they really want to change their lives.

The method I am teaching you is very simple. All you need to do is keep the intention and focus on repeating and memorizing the words that allow you to call back your power and realize that energy is the basis of all existence. To what extent you are present in your own life determines how much you can accomplish. If you are barely present, you can do and experience little. This causes a lot of people to give up or have a really hard time in life. If you are fully present, you can live the life your purpose intended.

Where is your energy going? If you are not in full possession of your power, then who has your power? You may not know what being in your power at one hundred percent feels like because you may never have experienced it. Therefore, you may think that sixty percent is one hundred percent. An example of this is when you experience an altitude change and your ears pop. Suddenly, you can hear much better, but before that moment, you hadn't realized that your hearing was compromised.

One of the best ways to truly know what it feels like to be in your full power is to consistently call all of your power back to you on a daily basis, then send the power that doesn't belong to you back from where you took it. Eventually, your system will come to the conclusion that you don't have to give your power away anymore.

Please read the previous sentence again, because that's where you are heading.

Sometimes we are unaware that we are giving our energies away and sometimes we are unaware that we are taking energies from others. For example, Mark 5:30-34 (Bible, NIV translation) states,

> *At once, Jesus realized that power had gone out from Him. He turned around in the crowd and asked, "Who touched my clothes?"*
>
> *"You see the people crowding against you," his disciples answered, "and yet you can ask, who touched me?"*
>
> *But Jesus kept looking around to see who had done it. Then the woman, knowing what had happened to her, came and fell at his feet, and trembling with fear, told him the whole truth. He said to her, "Daughter, your faith has healed you. Go in peace and be freed from suffering."*

This experience gives us insight into power and energy attitudes in general. It illustrates how to maintain power by activating the other person's system, to not let the parasitic approach succeed. How beautiful! Jesus said it was not his power but her faith that healed her. This is such a great example of inspiring others with your powerful insights without giving your power away in the process. He did not allow her to take power from him and run. Instead he claimed his power from her by reminding her of her own power of faith that healed her. He took his power back and reminded her of her own power in this case her power of faith.

Everybody has something to offer, nobody is without anything; we just have to be reminded sometimes to be activated again. Instead of creating an addicted beggar, Jesus activated her own power source.

Back to us now, let's say it together three times:

"I call all of my power back to me. I am whole and complete.
I call all of my power back to me. I am whole and complete.
I call all of my power back to me. I am whole and complete."

If you do not feel energy returning, repeat and reaffirm these words with greater intention. When energy returns, you will feel a tingling sensation throughout your body. It can become effortless to call your power back. Like a pet dog, it knows to return home. It will respond more strongly to its original owner.

This exercise is for anyone who wants to be more present and who desires to live life to the fullest potential. It is for those who are in possession of a small percentage of their power, and for those who are in ninety percent possession of their power. The focus and intention expressed in this exercise can change lives. An unmotivated person can turn into a successful person and jewel of a human being. Anyone can apply this system. I say anyone, but it is the person who desires to truly change who will benefit most from this exercise. That is why the consciousness beneath these words, which holds embedded wholeness frequencies, is crucial.

With the affirmations I shared with you earlier, I created a morphogenetic field that contains consciousness. Of course, the words still have to be applied. You still have to do and feel the exercise. When you say, "I call all of my power back to me. I am whole and complete," you will notice that the energy returning is distinct from simply saying the words.

Recall the highest spiritual experience you have ever had, perhaps an awakening moment, in church, meditating, chanting, or a visitation from God or the angels. The most amazing spiritual experience in a person's life is relatable to this exercise. My energy returning to me is often the most joyous, elating, even ecstatic experience, because my energy wants to be with me, and feel me, and flow with me. My power is comprised of pure life energy, the frequency of creation. All of my energies come back to me. I experience an energetic recharge.

This exercise can be as powerful as the most intense, loving, spiritual experience you have ever had, but it will also take you to the next higher level.

Daily repetition of the exercise is very important. Repeat this exercise daily fifty times for a minimum of ninety days. You are an unlimited energy system, and even if you called a lot of energy back yesterday, today you have to state and increase the focus because this Universe is ever expanding and new. You have to feel it and allow it to happen. Your power is not coming back to you if you do not feel that kind of energy. If you do not feel it, there is no power coming back.

When I say, "I call all of my power back to me. I am whole and complete," I call and send my intention of it out to the last corners of the Universe or Multiverse. Every aspect in the Multiverse hears me and sends my energy back because my energy wants to be with me and comply with my wishes. However, if I am not moving past the blockages or controlling forces that are holding my energies hostage somewhere, then how is my energy going to feel me and return to me?

If anybody holds your energy hostage in any dimension, and your intention is not strong enough to pass through that barrier to tell your energy to return to you, how can it return to you? You have to love your power more than anybody who loves your energy and keeps it. Close your eyes, Visualize the color of your power, and allow that energy light of your power to return to you now.

You really want the energy to return to you. Why? Because you love your power and you love to be powerful. It is vitally important for your life to be in possession of all of your power. Feeling that importance with all of your being is the focus that compels your energy, your power, to return to you. If you just say, "Hey, my energy, just come back to me," it says, "Hold on a second, I still have a few more things to do here."

It is your specific focus that really makes the return happen. Theoretically, anyone who wants your energy more than you want it could take it. It will go to the highest bidder! It will go to the person who believes, "I want this. I love this. I want to keep this." But in terms of power, your energy is more related to you than to anyone else. If you demand your energy back in a loving and firm way, then it will return to you.

Imagine being in really loud traffic in New York City and trying to call to someone you recognize on the other side of the street. You want them to hear you, so with how much intensity will you need to shout? With all the interference or background noise in the Universe, you want to make sure that your energy hears and understands that you want it to return, so express it energetically from your heart while speaking the words. Repeat this exercise fifty times daily for ninety days.

After firmly setting the intent, speak these words:

"I call all of my power back to me. I am whole and complete.
I call all of my power back to me. I am whole and complete.
I call all of my power back to me. I am whole and complete."

Do the hand movements laid out in chapter one to reinforce and intensify the words as you speak them. Your energy will hear you and return to you. This is an immediate activation. This will help the aspiring energy healer, the advanced, and everyone else, to really learn to be in full awareness, full consciousness, full potential, full energy, and full possession of our power.

CHAPTER 3

Imbalance of Relationship Energies

It is possible, at this moment, to freely but unintentionally give a lot of your life force to your current or even past partner(s). They do not have to be with you anymore in order to continue to receive your life force now and in the future. It is possible that your partner took energy from you without your permission because sometimes people are parasitic in relationships. People will not refrain from taking your energy even if they no longer share a physical space with you, as long as your energy remains freely available to them and makes them feel better. If it is an equal exchange, no worries. If it drains you, change has to happen or you get exhausted. In order for you to be in full control of all of your life force, you need to consciously stop allowing another person to drain your energy.

That means identifying the agreement made in the first place and recognizing when this takes place in daily life, then apply what you learned here. When your partner has a claim or entitlement on your life force, ask why is he or she more important in life than you? Why do you feel your partner needs more support than you in this moment and for what? If your (ex-) partner saves the planet, in this moment I understand. If your (ex-) partner uses your energy to create more imbalance for no healthy reasons, than think again what you're supporting.

It is time to take your power back and start living your healthy life. Create balance in your life with your current partner and you can both, be Living in power and in Love. This goes also for family and friend settings. Look and see. Without realistically addressing any stagnation or any interference, the message of people's desires or intentions will be unclear and then likely remain unanswered.

Think of a microscope or binoculars: several lenses have to be clear and aligned in order to see through to what we want to look at. Now compare yourself to the binoculars or the microscope that is focusing on God or the Universe—can you see it without interference? Your emotional, mental, spiritual, astral, and physical body has to be clear so the energy can flow unobstructed from you to the source and back from the source to you.

When you boost your focus and clarity with your power and energy-work on creating love and harmony. That's when you will break through old barriers and self-sabotaging patterns that have kept you from achieving your goals. Harmony means, very simply, that the inner child—Self and Higher Self—are in good alignment love flows freely. Your inner child, the Self and Higher Self, are very simple access points to who you are and what you manifest in your life. By aligning these aspects of your being, intentions are clearly expressed into the Universe. They're clearly expressed to the Universe, and clearly received by GOD and the Universe, because loving harmony has a very high value in the Universe.

If there is such a thing as the language of God, then it would be the **ideal spin and love harmony,** like the loving father- or mother-warming harmony of sacred geometrical patterns. It is understood as a Universal truth that since all life unfolds in the Fibonacci sequence, we humans are sacred geometry manifested and in motion. If all of our chakra systems are spinning and vibrating in harmony, we become a highlighted map, a destination that God and the Universe knows to deliver to us what we need.

CHAPTER 4.

Calling All of Your Life Force Back from Life-Suppressing Patterns and Emotions

Any negative and compulsive emotions or power struggles that recur on a daily basis can hold us hostage; they hold our life force hostage or hold our quality of life hostage. These emotions may be guilt, fear, anger, inadequacy, jealousy, or even road rage. Once you identify it, you can use the following exercise also for ninety days simultaneously with the previous ones. Do the hand motions while you speak the phrases.

Say out loud:

"I call all of my power and life force back to me that I have given to this emotion.

I call all of my power back to me. I am whole and complete.
I call all of my power back to me. I am whole and complete.
I call all of my power back to me. I am whole and complete."

When you are doing this work, you are changing your life. You are making yourself aware of what programs are running in your system, and then you are basically redirecting the energy and unplugging the mp3 player. The negative emotions stop repeating because they do not have any life force to keep going. If you want to create new healthier programs now, check out my book, *Sacred Inner Dialogue*, for easy scripts.

You always want to dig deeper. When working on yourself or when working with others, you might think, *how many times do I have to do this exercise?* Remember, giving our power away was a habit in the past, a pattern that has to be undone so a new pattern must be established. So, call your power back as often and as long as required, the more often the better, because you are teaching yourself to contain your power. Even if you think you are feeling really powerful today, think again, because you are an unlimited energy being, and compared to the infinite we can be infinitely more powerful.

The more often you call your power back, the more your system will prevent giving it away in the first place, because it understands that you want to contain your power at all times.

Once you see results, you will dig deeper and deeper. Systematically call your power back from the negative emotions, habits, patterns, trauma, or people that drain your power. When you are feeling a negative emotion, know that you are "paying" for this negative emotion with your life force. It is your life force, which you generate daily anew, that fuels this emotion. Check what triggers it. If you have multiple negative emotions that are depleting your life force simultaneously, that can greatly drain your life force to the extent that life can be a burden. If left unattended over a long period of time, these patterns and emotions can drain your life force and cause considerable imbalance. When our life force is parasitically drained, we frequently look for fast, unhealthy fuel outside of ourselves instead of recharging our own batteries and plugging ourselves back into our own

Power Source. Being constantly energetically drained is a life lived from deficiency instead of from a position of fullness and efficiency.

Continue the calling back of your power until you fully realize what your unhealthy drainers are, what their motivations are, and then call your life force and your power back from the very root cause of each of these unhealthy patterns. Then deal with them respectfully and know that deeper layers will still come up, because we are infinite energy beings.

Here are some modifications.

These changes in the beginnings of the exercise can also be utilized after some time of working with the original.

I call all of my power to me……

I call all of my power forward to me….

I call all of my power to me now….

Honor this technique and the words you are given to use as a process of reclaiming your own power. This process is whole in itself and of great benefit to your life. It allows you to live your life fully present and stay in your Power! OK?

To attend a *Calling Your Power Back to You* workshop, visit www.ataanahealingmethod.com and claim your space today!

DISCLAIMER

Self-healing is your own choice.

In the event of a medical emergency, call a doctor or 911 immediately.

This book is designed to provide information to my readers. No healing warranties or guarantees are expressed or implied by the author. The author shall not be liable for any physical, psychological, emotional, spiritual, financial, or commercial damages, including, but not limited to special, incidental, consequential, or other damages. Reading this book is your own choice and at your own risk.

It is sold with the understanding that the author is not engaged to render any type of medical, psychological, legal, or other advice.

This book is not intended to serve as a substitute for the consultation, diagnosis, and/or medical treatment of a qualified physician or healthcare provider.

Use sound judgment and be the best you can be at all times.